MARCILLINUS ASOGWA

Faith's Embrace: A Journey Beyond

This book was professionally typeset on Reedsy.
Find out more at reedsy.com

Contents

I

Part One

1

Whispers in the Dark

Father Gabriel stood in the dimly lit archive room of St. Mark's Cathedral, the air thick with the musty scent of old parchment and leather-bound volumes. The flickering candlelight cast eerie shadows on the walls, adding to the sense of unease that had settled over him since he had been assigned to catalog the ancient texts stored here. He could feel the weight of history pressing down on him, the whisper of forgotten voices carried on the dust motes that danced in the light.

Gabriel had always found solace in the quiet sanctity of the cathedral, but tonight was different. There was something unsettling about the silence, something that gnawed at the edges of his consciousness. He shook his head, trying to dispel the feeling as he turned his attention back to the task at hand. His fingers traced the spines of the books, seeking out the one he had been instructed to find: an ancient manuscript rumored to contain the lost writings of Saint Alaric, a revered figure whose prophecies had guided the church for centuries.

After what felt like hours of searching, Gabriel's hand finally brushed against a weathered, leather-bound volume tucked away on the highest shelf. He carefully pulled it down, his heart quickening as he examined the intricate, faded symbols embossed on the cover. This was it—the manuscript he had been seeking. He carried it to a nearby table, the wooden floorboards creaking underfoot, and gently laid it down.

As Gabriel opened the manuscript, a chill ran down his spine. The pages were brittle with age, filled with dense, spidery script and elaborate illustrations. His eyes scanned the text, struggling to decipher the archaic Latin. Suddenly, a word caught his attention: "prophecy." His breath hitched as he read on, the ominous nature of the text becoming clear.

"The time of reckoning shall come," it began, "when the shadows of the past rise to consume the light. Only those of true faith shall stand against the darkness, armed with the relic of the first martyr." Gabriel's hands trembled as he turned the page, revealing a detailed illustration of a mysterious artifact—a relic that he had never seen before.

The sound of footsteps echoed through the corridor outside, startling Gabriel from his intense concentration. He quickly closed the manuscript and hid it beneath a pile of old texts. The door creaked open, and Sister Maria stepped into the room, her eyes widening as she took in Gabriel's disheveled appearance.

"Father Gabriel, are you all right?" she asked, her voice tinged with concern.

Gabriel forced a smile, though he could still feel the weight of the prophecy pressing on his mind. "I'm fine, Sister Maria. Just... lost in my work."

Maria's gaze fell on the pile of books on the table. "Did you find what you were looking for?"

Gabriel hesitated for a moment before nodding. "Yes, I did. But I need your help to understand it fully."

Maria's curiosity was piqued. She had always been intrigued by the church's history and the mysteries it held. "Of course, Father. What did you find?"

Gabriel took a deep breath and retrieved the manuscript from its hiding place. "This," he said, placing it on the table. "It's an ancient prophecy, one that speaks of a time of great darkness and a relic that can stop it."

Maria's eyes widened as she read the text. "This is incredible," she whispered. "But what does it mean? And why was it hidden away?"

"I don't know," Gabriel admitted. "But I have a feeling that we were meant to find it now, at this moment. We need to decipher the rest of the manuscript and find out more about this relic."

Maria nodded, her expression resolute. "Then let's get to work. We don't have a moment to lose."

As they pored over the manuscript together, a sense of urgency filled the room. The prophecy's warnings were clear, but the path to understanding and preventing the impending catastrophe was shrouded in mystery. Gabriel and Maria knew that their faith and determination would be tested in the days to come, but they were ready to face whatever challenges lay ahead.

Outside the archive room, the cathedral was cloaked in darkness, the moonlight casting an ethereal glow through the stained glass windows. The whispers in the dark seemed to grow louder, echoing the secrets that had been unearthed and the dangers that awaited. The journey beyond was about to begin, and with it, the fate of their faith hung in the balance.

2

The Forbidden Texts

The air in the cathedral felt thick with anticipation as Father Gabriel and Sister Maria gathered their notes around the old oak table in the dim light of the archive. A sense of urgency tinged every word they exchanged, the ancient manuscript lying open before them like a gateway to hidden truths. Gabriel's fingers danced over the pages, tracing the elegant yet cryptic script of Saint Alaric, his mind racing to decode the chilling prophecy they had unearthed.

Maria leaned closer, her brow furrowing in concentration. "What do you think this 'relic of the first martyr' refers to?" she asked, her voice barely above a whisper. "Is it a physical object, or something more abstract?"

Gabriel shook his head, feeling the weight of her question. "I wish I knew. If it's a relic, it must hold some kind of power—something that can protect against the darkness the text warns of." His thoughts drifted to the vivid illustrations, which depicted the relic surrounded by swirling shadows and light, as if to suggest an eternal battle between good and evil.

A cold draft swept through the room, causing the candles to flicker wildly. Maria glanced towards the door, her instincts telling her that they were not alone. "Do you hear that?" she asked, her voice trembling slightly.

Gabriel strained to listen. For a moment, he heard nothing but the soft rustling of pages. Then, just as he was about to dismiss her concern, a faint whisper echoed from the corridor outside—an indistinguishable murmur that sent shivers down his spine.

"Stay here," Gabriel instructed, rising from his chair. He moved cautiously toward the door, each step heavy with the weight of impending dread. He placed a hand on the cold, wooden door and paused, listening intently. The whispering continued, growing more distinct yet remaining elusive, like an echo of a forgotten conversation.

Just as he was about to push the door open, it creaked inward. A figure stood silhouetted in the doorway, casting a long shadow across the room. Gabriel's heart raced as he recognized the man—the church's historian, Father Anton, who was known for his deep knowledge of the faith's hidden truths but also for his enigmatic demeanor.

"Father Gabriel," Anton said, his voice smooth yet laced with an underlying tension. "I was hoping to find you here."

"What do you want?" Gabriel replied, feeling a surge of suspicion. There was something off about Anton's presence, a subtle undercurrent of urgency that raised alarm bells in Gabriel's mind.

"I've heard whispers—rumors about your recent discoveries in the archives," Anton said, his eyes darting towards the manuscript on the table. "It's imperative that you tell me everything you've found."

Gabriel exchanged a glance with Maria, who had remained seated, her expression a mixture of curiosity and caution. "We've uncovered a prophecy that speaks of a coming darkness and a relic that can stop it," Gabriel said, choosing his words carefully. "But we don't fully understand it yet."

Anton stepped into the room, his face obscured in shadows, but Gabriel could see the gleam of excitement in his eyes. "You must be careful," he warned, lowering his voice. "There are those who would do anything to keep such knowledge hidden. The church has secrets that can shake the very foundations of our faith."

A chill swept through Gabriel, but he held his ground. "What do you know about it, Father Anton?"

"The relic is more than just an object; it's a key—a conduit of faith that has been protected for centuries. But if the wrong hands get hold of it, it could unleash chaos," Anton said, his tone growing more intense. "You're playing with forces you don't yet understand."

Gabriel felt a surge of anger at Anton's cryptic warning. "If there's a threat, we need to confront it, not hide in the shadows. We owe it to the congregation to protect them."

Anton smirked, the shadow of his smile revealing a hint of something darker. "And how far are you willing to go, Father? Are you prepared to face the consequences of uncovering forbidden texts?"

Before Gabriel could respond, Maria interjected, her voice steady. "We will do what is right. We can't ignore the prophecy just because it makes us uncomfortable."

Anton's expression hardened, and the atmosphere in the room shifted, becoming suffocatingly tense. "Very well. Just remember, curiosity can lead to peril. There are forces at work in the world that are beyond your comprehension." With that, he turned on his heel and strode out of the room, leaving Gabriel and Maria in a heavy silence.

"What was that all about?" Maria asked, her brow furrowed in concern. "Do you think he knows more than he's letting on?"

"I don't trust him," Gabriel admitted, running a hand through his hair. "He seems too invested in keeping us from discovering the truth. But we can't let fear dictate our actions."

As they returned to their notes, the atmosphere felt charged with a new urgency. Maria began flipping through the manuscript, searching for any additional clues that could lead them to the relic. "If this relic truly exists, we need to find it before anyone else does."

"Agreed," Gabriel replied, his mind racing with possibilities. "The manuscript might hold more secrets, more connections to our past. We have to decipher every word."

Just then, the distant sound of footsteps echoed through the corridor again, louder this time, growing closer with every heartbeat. Gabriel and Maria exchanged worried glances.

"Do you think it's Anton?" Maria whispered, her eyes wide with fear.

"Or someone else," Gabriel replied, the weight of their discovery pressing down on him. They quickly gathered the manuscript and their notes, hiding them beneath the table as the footsteps drew nearer.

Just as they finished concealing their work, the door swung open again, revealing a cloaked figure with a hood drawn low over their face. The stranger's presence radiated an unsettling energy, sending a chill through Gabriel's spine.

"Father Gabriel, Sister Maria," the figure said, their voice smooth and calm, yet filled with an unnerving intensity. "We need to talk about the prophecy.

Time is of the essence."

Gabriel's heart raced as he took a step forward, every instinct screaming that they were now entangled in something far beyond their initial understanding. The night had only just begun, and the shadows were closing in fast.

3

Echoes of the Past

The flickering candlelight cast elongated shadows against the cold stone walls of St. Mark's Cathedral as Father Gabriel and Sister Maria sat at the old oak table, the tension thick enough to cut with a knife. The cloaked figure, whose face remained hidden in the darkness, shifted slightly, drawing the attention of both Gabriel and Maria.

"Who are you?" Gabriel demanded, his voice steady despite the unease knotting in his stomach. "What do you know about the prophecy?"

The figure lowered their hood, revealing a face that seemed oddly familiar yet foreign. Deep-set eyes gleamed with an intensity that made Gabriel's pulse quicken. "My name is Elara. I've come to help you." Her voice was low and resonant, carrying an edge of urgency.

"Help us?" Maria echoed skeptically. "And why should we trust you?"

Elara leaned forward, her hands clasped together, revealing fingers adorned with intricate silver rings etched with ancient symbols. "Because the time for secrets is over. The prophecy you've uncovered is not just words on a page.

It's a living thing, and it has begun to awaken."

Gabriel exchanged a glance with Maria. The weight of her statement hung in the air, making the shadows dance more fervently. "What do you mean by 'awaken'?" Gabriel asked, his curiosity mingling with suspicion.

"The darkness spoken of in the prophecy is rising. There are forces—powers that have long lain dormant—that are now stirring," Elara explained, her eyes darting to the door as if expecting an intruder. "And they will stop at nothing to claim the relic."

Gabriel felt a shiver run down his spine. "The relic of the first martyr. You know where it is?"

Elara hesitated, glancing back at the door again, her brow furrowing. "I have an idea, but we need to act quickly. You must understand the significance of the relic. It is not merely a physical object; it is a key to something far greater."

Maria leaned forward, intrigued despite her apprehensions. "What do you mean by 'greater'?"

"The relic holds the power to seal away the darkness," Elara replied, her voice barely above a whisper. "But it has been hidden for centuries, protected by a sect of monks who have sworn to guard its secret. They were the original keepers of the prophecy."

"And how do you know all of this?" Gabriel pressed, trying to gauge her sincerity.

"My family has served the church for generations," Elara said, her gaze unwavering. "For years, we have studied the ancient texts and followed the whispers of our ancestors. We have always known this day would come."

Before Gabriel could respond, a loud crash echoed from the entrance of the cathedral, causing them all to freeze. The sound of hurried footsteps echoed through the hallowed halls, each step growing closer, reverberating in Gabriel's chest. "We're not safe here," he whispered urgently. "We need to go."

Elara nodded, her demeanor shifting from calm to urgent. "Follow me. There's a hidden passage that leads to the old catacombs beneath the cathedral. It's our only chance."

With no time to waste, Gabriel and Maria exchanged a determined glance before following Elara through the narrow corridor that led to the catacombs. The air grew colder as they descended, the walls lined with age-old stones slick with moisture. The flickering candlelight barely illuminated their path, casting grotesque shapes that seemed to shift and move with each breath they took.

"Stay close," Gabriel instructed, feeling the weight of the darkness surrounding them. Every echo of their footsteps was amplified, creating an unsettling chorus of sounds that made his heart race. He could feel the ominous presence of something watching them, lurking just beyond the reach of their light.

As they reached the bottom of the stairs, the passage opened into a vast underground chamber. The air was heavy with the scent of earth and decay, and the walls were lined with niches that held the remains of long-forgotten saints. In the center of the room stood a stone altar, its surface covered in dust and cobwebs, yet it radiated an energy that set Gabriel's teeth on edge.

"What is this place?" Maria breathed, her eyes wide with wonder and fear.

"This is the burial site of the original guardians of the relic," Elara explained, her voice echoing in the cavernous space. "They were the first to protect the prophecy, and they built this catacomb as a sanctuary."

Gabriel stepped closer to the altar, running his fingers along its rough surface. "But where is the relic?" he asked, scanning the room for any signs or clues.

Elara's eyes darkened as she surveyed the chamber. "It's here, somewhere among these remains. The guardians hid it well to prevent it from falling into the wrong hands."

Just then, a chilling draft swept through the chamber, causing the candles to flicker violently. Gabriel's instincts flared, and he turned sharply towards the entrance. "We need to hurry," he said, his voice taut with urgency.

As they began to search the niches for any signs of the relic, Gabriel felt a surge of determination. The whispers of the past echoed in his mind, urging him onward. With each moment, the darkness outside felt closer, more oppressive, as if it were a living entity waiting for its moment to strike.

"I think I found something!" Maria exclaimed, her voice breaking the tension as she crouched beside an ornate sarcophagus adorned with symbols of the first martyr.

Gabriel rushed over, his heart pounding as he knelt beside her. The lid was slightly ajar, revealing a faint glow emanating from within. As Maria reached in, her fingers brushed against something cool and metallic.

"Be careful!" Gabriel warned, the hairs on the back of his neck standing on end.

With a steady hand, Maria grasped the object and pulled it from the sarcophagus. It was a small, intricately designed box, adorned with silver and gold inlays that shimmered in the dim light. The air around them seemed to crackle with energy, and Gabriel could feel the weight of destiny resting on their shoulders.

As Maria opened the box, a blinding light erupted from within, illuminating the catacombs and casting away the shadows that had cloaked them. Gabriel shielded his eyes, his heart racing as he caught a glimpse of the relic—a crystal chalice, radiant and ethereal, pulsating with an otherworldly glow.

"This is it," he breathed, awe-struck. "This is the relic."

But before they could fully process their discovery, a loud crash echoed through the chamber, reverberating off the stone walls. The entrance was suddenly filled with figures cloaked in darkness, their faces obscured. The leader stepped forward, the glint of a dagger catching the light as he raised it high.

"We've found you," the leader sneered, a sinister grin spreading across his face. "And now, we will take what is ours."

Gabriel's heart raced as he turned to Elara and Maria, a mixture of fear and determination coursing through him. The darkness had indeed come, and they were standing at the precipice of a battle that would determine the fate of their faith and the world itself. The echoes of the past were no longer whispers; they had become a deafening roar.

4

The Hidden Key

The air in the catacombs felt charged with tension, the remnants of ancient echoes mixing with the heavy breaths of Gabriel, Maria, and Elara as they faced the cloaked figures blocking their escape. Gabriel could feel the relic pulsing gently in Maria's hands, its glow illuminating the ominous presence before them. The leader of the dark figures, his face partially obscured by a hood, stepped closer, his dagger glinting menacingly in the dim light.

"You have something that belongs to us," the leader said, his voice low and gravelly. "Hand over the chalice, and perhaps we'll allow you to live."

Maria instinctively tightened her grip on the relic, her knuckles turning white as panic coursed through her veins. "We will never give it to you," she replied, her voice steady despite the fear gnawing at her insides.

Gabriel felt a surge of protectiveness as he placed himself between Maria and the encroaching danger. "You don't understand what you're dealing with," he said, his voice firm. "This chalice is not just an object; it holds the key to stopping the darkness that you serve."

The leader let out a low, mocking laugh, sending a chill down Gabriel's spine. "Oh, I understand perfectly, Father. But you see, the darkness is not something to be feared. It is the truth that your precious faith has hidden away for too long."

"Enough!" Elara interjected, her voice rising above the tension in the chamber. "You think you can take the chalice, but it is protected by forces you cannot comprehend. Leave now, and you might just escape with your lives."

The leader's expression shifted, a flicker of annoyance crossing his face. "You're brave, girl, but bravery will not save you. You've stepped into a world you don't belong to." With a swift motion, he gestured to his companions, and they began to advance, closing in on Gabriel and Maria.

"Now!" Gabriel shouted, taking a step back and positioning himself closer to Maria, determined to shield her. "We need to get out of here!"

In a heartbeat, Gabriel felt a rush of adrenaline, the instinct to protect his allies overriding the fear that threatened to paralyze him. He glanced around the chamber, desperate for a way out. The ancient stones loomed overhead like a silent witness to the impending confrontation. Without thinking, he raised his voice, reciting a verse from the scripture that had always held power over darkness. "The light shall shine in the darkness, and the darkness shall not overcome it!"

As the words left his lips, a brilliant light erupted from the chalice in Maria's hands, bathing the chamber in an ethereal glow. The cloaked figures faltered, momentarily blinded by the radiance. Gabriel seized the moment, grabbing Maria's arm. "Now! We have to go!"

They dashed towards a narrow passage at the far end of the chamber, the sounds of their pursuers crashing behind them. The walls felt alive, closing in as they ran, but the light from the chalice guided their path, illuminating the way through the twisting catacombs.

"Where does this lead?" Maria gasped, her breath coming in quick bursts as they navigated the labyrinth of stone.

"Old tunnels," Elara explained, glancing back to ensure they weren't being followed. "They were used centuries ago to transport the relics. If we can reach the exit, we might be able to lose them."

But as they turned another corner, Gabriel skidded to a halt. Before them stood a heavy iron door, its surface etched with intricate symbols, some of which matched those on the chalice. "What now?" Maria asked, panic lacing her voice as the sounds of their pursuers grew louder behind them.

"This door must be the way out," Gabriel said, stepping closer. "But how do we open it?"

Elara examined the door, her fingers tracing the symbols with reverence. "These symbols... they're a form of ancient language. They represent the elements—earth, air, fire, and water. We must align the chalice with the symbols to unlock it."

The sound of footsteps grew closer, urgency thickening the air. "We don't have time for that!" Gabriel urged, his heart racing as he felt the pressure mounting. "Can't we just force it open?"

"No! That could trigger a trap," Elara replied, her voice steady but insistent. "Trust me. We need to do this correctly."

Gabriel took a deep breath, glancing at Maria. "We can do this. Just focus." He felt the warmth of the chalice in Maria's grip, a reminder of the hope it symbolized. "What do we need to do?"

"Place the chalice against each symbol in the order of the elements," Elara instructed. "Start with earth, then water, air, and finally fire. It must be done precisely."

"Let's do it," Maria said, determination gleaming in her eyes. "We can't let them catch us."

Gabriel nodded, and together, they positioned themselves in front of the door. As Maria held the chalice high, Gabriel guided her to the first symbol representing earth. She pressed the chalice against it, and the moment the chalice made contact, a deep rumble echoed through the chamber. The door shuddered, the symbols glowing faintly in response to the relic's presence.

"Now water!" Elara urged, her eyes wide with hope.

Maria swiftly moved the chalice to the symbol of water. The moment it touched, a cascade of light erupted, illuminating the room in brilliant hues. The door trembled even more violently, and Gabriel could feel the air crackle with energy.

"Quickly! Air!" Gabriel shouted, his heart racing as he glanced back, hearing the footsteps of their pursuers nearing.

They moved to the symbol of air. As Maria pressed the chalice against it, a whirlwind of wind swept through the chamber, swirling around them like a protective barrier. The door's vibration intensified, resonating with the power of the chalice.

"Last one! Fire!" Elara urged, her voice filled with urgency.

With a final surge of determination, Maria placed the chalice against the fire symbol. In an instant, flames erupted around the door, dancing in a controlled frenzy. The heat surged, forcing the air to shimmer, and with one last resounding crack, the door swung open.

"Go!" Gabriel shouted, shoving Maria forward. "Get through!"

They rushed through the doorway, tumbling into a narrow tunnel that spiraled upwards, the light from the chalice illuminating their path. Behind them, the air crackled with tension, and Gabriel could hear the angry shouts of their pursuers echoing in the depths of the catacombs.

"Keep going!" he urged, adrenaline fueling their escape. They sprinted up the tunnel, the walls closing in around them as they ascended, each step taking them closer to the surface and, hopefully, safety.

At the top of the tunnel, a faint light began to filter through the cracks in the stone, guiding them forward. With a final push, they reached the end, bursting through a hidden exit into the night air.

They stumbled into a small clearing, surrounded by the towering trees of the cathedral's grounds. Gabriel gasped for breath, taking a moment to collect himself. The cool night air felt like a balm against the heat of the chase, but they couldn't linger.

"Where do we go now?" Maria asked, looking around frantically.

"Anywhere but here," Gabriel replied, glancing back toward the tunnel entrance, knowing their pursuers would not be far behind. "We need to regroup and figure out our next move."

Elara's expression was serious, her eyes scanning the shadows around them. "We can't stay exposed. There's an old chapel nearby that has been abandoned for years. It should provide some cover."

"Lead the way," Gabriel said, and together, they set off into the woods, the weight of the chalice heavy in Maria's hands. The forest seemed alive with whispers, shadows flickering in the moonlight as they made their way deeper into the trees.

With each step, the darkness loomed ever closer, and Gabriel could feel the echoes of the past pressing down on them, the weight of destiny intertwining with the threads of their faith. The hidden key had been uncovered, but the battle was far from over.

5

Shadows in the Chapel

The dense forest loomed around them, branches intertwining like skeletal fingers reaching out from the darkness. As Gabriel, Maria, and Elara hurried toward the old chapel, the night was alive with sounds—the rustling of leaves, the distant hoot of an owl, and the relentless crunch of twigs underfoot. Every noise seemed amplified in the eerie quiet of the woods, sending tremors of unease through Gabriel's heart.

"Are we sure this chapel is safe?" Maria whispered, her voice barely above a breath as they navigated the thick underbrush. Her grip on the chalice remained tight, as if it were a lifeline in the encroaching darkness.

"It's the best chance we have," Elara replied, glancing over her shoulder. "The old chapel is hidden from the main paths. If we can reach it, we can regroup and plan our next move."

Gabriel felt a surge of doubt but didn't voice it. The palpable tension in the air weighed heavily on his chest. He could sense that danger was still lurking, the cloaked figures hunting them like predators in the night. "We need to hurry," he urged, pushing through a thicket of bushes that snagged at his clothes.

They pressed onward, the silhouettes of the trees casting long, ominous shadows that danced with each flicker of light from the chalice. Gabriel's mind raced with the enormity of their situation—the prophecy, the relic, and the darkness they had awakened.

Suddenly, they emerged into a small clearing, and there it stood—the old chapel, a crumbling relic of a bygone era. Its stone façade was mottled with age, vines creeping up its sides like the fingers of time trying to reclaim it. The wooden door hung ajar, creaking softly in the breeze, as if inviting them to enter.

"Here it is," Elara said, her voice a mixture of relief and caution. "Let's go inside."

They hurried toward the chapel, glancing around for any signs of pursuit. Gabriel pushed the door open wider, revealing a dimly lit interior. The air was thick with dust, and the faint scent of mildew lingered, a testament to years of neglect. Wooden pews lined the walls, some overturned, while shattered stained glass windows cast fragmented rainbows across the stone floor.

"Check for any windows or exits," Gabriel instructed, his voice steady despite the pounding of his heart. "We can't be too careful."

As Maria moved toward the back, Gabriel felt a prickle of awareness at the nape of his neck, an instinctive warning that danger was closer than they realized. He turned his attention to Elara, who was studying the walls adorned with faded murals of saints and angels. "Do you think they can find us here?" he asked, his voice low.

"They could," Elara replied, her brow furrowed in thought. "But if we remain quiet and hidden, we may have time to gather our thoughts."

Just then, Maria's voice echoed from the back of the chapel. "Gabriel! You need to see this!"

Gabriel exchanged a worried glance with Elara before rushing toward the sound. He found Maria kneeling beside a small altar, her face pale. "Look," she whispered, pointing to the floor.

The wooden floorboards had been pushed aside, revealing a trapdoor leading down into darkness. Gabriel's pulse quickened as he approached, kneeling beside Maria to examine it. The door was old and covered in dust, but it seemed sturdy enough. "What do you think is down there?" he asked, his voice low.

"I don't know," Maria replied, biting her lip. "But it could be a way to escape if they find us."

"We can't take that risk," Elara cautioned, glancing back toward the entrance. "We don't know what we'll encounter if we go down there."

Gabriel hesitated, his mind racing. "What if there's something down there? Something that can help us?"

A noise from outside broke their concentration—a snapping twig, the unmistakable sound of footsteps. Gabriel's heart sank as he exchanged worried glances with Maria and Elara. "They're here," he hissed, panic creeping into his voice.

"Quick! We need to decide," Maria urged, her eyes wide with fear.

"Down," Gabriel said, his voice firm. "If we stay here, we'll be trapped. We have to take our chances." He grabbed the trapdoor handle and pulled it open, revealing a dark staircase leading down into an abyss.

"Are you sure?" Elara asked, her eyes darting between the entrance and the opening.

"Now!" Gabriel urged, pushing Maria gently toward the trapdoor. She hesitated for a moment before nodding, her determination returning.

They descended into the darkness, the air growing cooler as they moved deeper. The sound of their footsteps echoed ominously in the narrow space, the darkness swallowing them whole. Gabriel could feel the weight of their situation pressing down, the fear of the unknown gnawing at him.

At the bottom of the stairs, they emerged into a small chamber illuminated by the faint glow from the chalice. The walls were lined with stone, damp and cold, and the air was thick with the scent of earth. In the center of the room stood an ancient stone table, covered in dust and strewn with fragments of what appeared to be old manuscripts and relics.

"What is this place?" Maria whispered, glancing around in awe and trepidation.

"I don't know, but it looks like it hasn't been touched in ages," Gabriel replied, stepping closer to the table. He picked up one of the scrolls, carefully unfurling it. The script was faded but legible, filled with sketches of the relics and detailed descriptions of their powers.

"Gabriel, look at this!" Maria exclaimed, holding up a small dagger that shimmered in the light of the chalice. "This could be useful!"

"Be careful with that!" Elara warned, her voice rising as she joined them. "We don't know what it might hold. It could be cursed or—"

But before she could finish her sentence, the sound of footsteps thundered above them, the floorboards creaking ominously. The heavy thud of boots reverberated in the chamber, sending a jolt of fear through Gabriel.

"Get down!" he hissed, shoving Maria and Elara behind the table as he instinctively reached for the dagger. His heart raced as the footsteps grew louder, echoing ominously through the chamber.

"What do we do?" Maria whispered, her voice trembling as she clutched the chalice close.

"We wait," Gabriel replied, his breath shallow. "If they come down here, we'll have to be ready."

The footsteps above ceased, and an unsettling silence enveloped them. Gabriel's heart thundered in his chest, every instinct screaming for him to flee. The shadows danced menacingly as the light from the chalice flickered, casting eerie shapes against the walls.

Suddenly, a loud crash sounded from above, and the trapdoor burst open. A figure loomed in the entrance, silhouetted against the dim light. "They've gone down here!" the leader shouted, his voice echoing through the chamber. "Search everywhere!"

Panic surged through Gabriel as he realized they had mere moments before they would be discovered. "Get ready!" he whispered, gripping the dagger tightly as he positioned himself behind the stone table, adrenaline coursing through his veins.

The figure began to descend, his silhouette growing clearer as he stepped into the chamber. Gabriel's breath caught in his throat as he prepared to fight, the weight of the dagger a comforting reminder of the stakes. He could hear his heart pounding in his ears, the air thick with tension.

Then, without warning, the leader turned, glancing around the chamber. "They must be here!" he growled, stepping further into the darkness.

Gabriel's mind raced, every thought focused on the impending confrontation. He could hear the rustle of fabric, the sound of breath. The dagger felt heavy in his grip, but he was ready to protect his friends, ready to fight for the relic and their lives.

"Now!" Gabriel shouted, lunging from behind the table as he brandished the dagger. The leader's eyes widened in surprise, but he quickly regained his composure, drawing a weapon of his own.

"Fools!" he spat, lunging forward with a snarl, but Gabriel was faster. The dagger glinted in the dim light as he slashed, the blade connecting with the leader's arm.

A fierce cry of pain erupted from the figure as he stumbled back, clutching his wound. Gabriel's heart raced with adrenaline, knowing they were in a fight for their lives.

"Run!" he shouted to Maria and Elara, who stood frozen for a moment, shock and fear etched on their faces. "Now!"

They sprang into action, scrambling to their feet as Gabriel continued to fend off the leader, dodging blows and keeping the man at bay.

The chamber erupted into chaos, shadows colliding with light, the air thick with the scent of fear and determination. As Gabriel fought with everything he had, he knew that the outcome of this battle would determine the fate of their mission and the darkness that loomed just beyond the chapel. The shadows were closing in, but they would not go down without a fight.

6

The Gathering Storm

The air in the chapel was thick with tension as Gabriel, Maria, and Elara regrouped after the chaotic confrontation. The flickering light from the chalice bathed the ancient stones in a soft, golden hue, but it did little to ease the gnawing dread settling in Gabriel's gut. They had fought hard, but the shadows were relentless, and the leader's ominous words echoed in his mind—"You cannot defeat the darkness; it is all-consuming."

"Do you think he's gone for good?" Maria asked, her voice barely above a whisper. She was still clutching the chalice, its warm glow providing a sense of comfort, but Gabriel could see the tremor in her hands.

"I don't know," Gabriel replied, forcing his thoughts to focus. "But we can't stay here. We need to move, find a safer place to regroup." He looked at Elara, whose face was set in determination, her eyes scanning the dim chamber for any signs of danger.

"Let's check the exit," Elara said, stepping toward the trapdoor they had come through. "If they're still searching above, we might be able to find another way out."

They quickly made their way back to the trapdoor, Gabriel leading the way. He lifted the heavy door and peered into the darkness above. The chapel was still silent, but the feeling of being watched lingered in the air. He could feel the weight of uncertainty pressing down on him.

"Do you hear that?" Maria asked, her voice tense. Gabriel strained his ears, listening intently. There it was—the faintest sound of footsteps echoing from above, muffled yet unmistakable.

"We need to hurry," Gabriel urged, glancing back at Maria and Elara. "We can't afford to be caught off guard again."

Elara nodded, and they quickly climbed up the stairs, the trapdoor creaking ominously under their weight. Gabriel pushed the door open cautiously, scanning the chapel for any signs of movement. The flickering light from the chalice illuminated the room, but the corners remained cloaked in shadow, hiding potential threats.

"Looks clear," he said, stepping inside and beckoning Maria and Elara to follow. The three of them entered the chapel, the heavy door creaking shut behind them with an echo that sent a chill down Gabriel's spine.

They moved cautiously toward the main entrance, Gabriel's heart pounding as he pushed open the door just enough to peek outside. The moon hung high in the sky, casting silvery beams across the forest. The trees loomed like sentinels, their branches swaying gently in the night breeze, but the path leading away from the chapel seemed eerily quiet.

"Where do we go from here?" Maria asked, anxiety creeping into her voice. "What if they're still out there?"

"We have to stick together," Gabriel said, stepping fully outside. He scanned the area, listening for any sounds that might indicate they were being hunted.

"There's a small village not far from here. If we can reach it, we can regroup and find help."

"Lead the way," Elara said, her determination evident. They moved as a unit, keeping close to the walls of the chapel, staying low and silent as they made their way into the cover of the trees.

As they ventured deeper into the forest, a sense of unease settled over them like a thick fog. Every rustle of leaves and snap of twigs set Gabriel's heart racing, but they pressed on, the fear of the unknown propelling them forward. The shadows cast by the moon danced eerily around them, and Gabriel couldn't shake the feeling that something was lurking just beyond the light.

"Do you think the others made it out?" Maria asked, breaking the silence that had enveloped them. "What if they didn't?"

Gabriel's mind flashed to their companions, the other seekers who had joined them in the quest to retrieve the chalice. "They're strong," he replied, trying to instill some hope. "If anyone can survive, it's them. But we can't dwell on that now. We need to focus on getting to safety."

As they continued their trek through the underbrush, Gabriel felt a shift in the air. A cold breeze swept through the trees, rustling the leaves ominously. Suddenly, he heard it—a low growl, deep and resonant, echoing from somewhere in the darkness ahead.

"Did you hear that?" Elara asked, her voice tense.

Gabriel nodded, instinctively gripping the dagger tighter in his hand. "Stay close. We might not be alone."

They advanced slowly, every sense heightened as they navigated through the thickening trees. The growl grew louder, reverberating through the night, and

Gabriel felt a knot of fear twist in his stomach. Whatever was lurking in the shadows was not far away.

Then, without warning, a massive figure lunged from the underbrush. Gabriel barely had time to react as a monstrous wolf, its eyes glowing with an otherworldly light, charged toward them. He instinctively stepped in front of Maria and Elara, raising his dagger just as the beast lunged at him.

The wolf was enormous, its fur dark as night, and it snarled menacingly, showing teeth that gleamed like daggers in the moonlight. Gabriel's heart raced as he faced the creature, the instinct to fight mingling with a primal fear.

"Back! Get back!" he shouted to Maria and Elara, his voice steady despite the chaos around him. He sidestepped the beast's powerful jaws, narrowly avoiding its snap as it lunged at him again.

"Gabriel!" Maria cried, her voice shaking. "What do we do?"

"Stay behind me!" he barked, his mind racing for a plan. He couldn't let the creature attack them. It was as if the shadows themselves had manifested into this beast, a dark omen of what lay ahead.

The wolf circled them, its growls reverberating through the air. Gabriel's mind raced; he had to distract it. He could feel the energy of the chalice pulsing behind him, and suddenly, a thought struck him. "Maria! The chalice! Use it!"

Without hesitation, Maria raised the chalice high, its light spilling out in a brilliant wave. The wolf paused, its growls faltering as it seemed to recoil from the radiant glow. "In the name of faith, I command you to leave!" Maria shouted, her voice strong despite her fear.

Gabriel felt the surge of power emanating from the chalice, and he instinctively moved closer to Maria, hoping to use the light to their advantage. "Keep it steady!" he urged. "Focus on the light!"

The wolf snarled, advancing again, but the light from the chalice pushed against the darkness, illuminating the area around them. Gabriel could see the creature more clearly now, its eyes filled with rage and confusion, but also something else—a flicker of uncertainty.

"Gabriel, what if it's not enough?" Elara whispered, fear gripping her.

"It has to be!" he replied, determination surging within him. He took a step forward, brandishing his dagger, and shouted, "You are not of this realm! Return to the shadows!"

The wolf hesitated, its growl faltering as it seemed to feel the power of the chalice washing over it. Gabriel could see the struggle within its eyes, the fierce loyalty to the darkness battling against the light before it.

Then, with a sudden burst of energy, the wolf lunged again, but this time it was different. It was as if the creature had lost its ferocity, driven more by instinct than aggression. Gabriel raised the dagger, ready to defend himself, but Maria held the chalice steady, its glow piercing through the gloom.

"Stay back!" Gabriel warned, but the wolf halted just inches from him, its breath heavy and labored. It was caught between two worlds, the darkness and the light, and Gabriel could sense that the chalice was having an effect.

The creature hesitated, its growl dying down to a low whimper. For a moment, Gabriel felt an overwhelming surge of compassion for the beast. It wasn't just a creature of the shadows; it was a victim, perhaps as lost as they were.

"Please, we mean you no harm," Maria said, her voice gentle yet firm. "We're not your enemies."

The wolf's eyes softened, confusion giving way to a flicker of understanding. Slowly, it backed away, retreating into the shadows from whence it came, the darkness folding around it like a shroud.

Gabriel exhaled sharply, lowering his dagger. "Is it... gone?" he asked, his voice shaky.

"I think so," Elara replied, glancing around nervously. "But we need to move. There's no telling what else might be lurking in the shadows."

"Right," Gabriel said, glancing back at Maria, who still held the chalice. "We have to keep going. The village is close; we just need to make it through the forest."

They continued their journey, the tension lingering in the air but gradually dissipating with each step. Gabriel kept his gaze focused ahead, his heart still racing from the encounter. He knew they had escaped the wolf, but he couldn't shake the feeling that the darkness was gathering, preparing for another strike.

As they pushed through the underbrush, the sound of distant voices began to filter through the trees, a beacon of hope in the otherwise oppressive silence. Gabriel felt a surge of relief; the village was near.

"Do you hear that?" Maria whispered, her eyes wide with anticipation.

"Let's go," Gabriel urged, quickening his pace. They moved with renewed determination, the light from the chalice guiding their

7

The Village of Shadows

The faint sounds of laughter and chatter grew louder as Gabriel, Maria, and Elara emerged from the dense foliage, stepping into a clearing that revealed the village nestled at the edge of the forest. The moon hung high in the sky, illuminating the quaint homes with its silver glow, but the warm glow of lanterns flickered in the windows, beckoning them closer.

"Is it safe?" Elara whispered, glancing nervously over her shoulder. The woods felt alive, as if the shadows were watching their every move, and Gabriel could feel the weight of the darkness pressing against them.

"It has to be," Gabriel replied, trying to reassure them. "We can't stop now."

They approached the first house, its thatched roof lined with blooming vines and flowers that swayed gently in the breeze. The vibrant colors felt oddly comforting after the oppressive darkness of the forest, but Gabriel remained alert, scanning the surroundings for any signs of trouble.

"Let's knock," Maria suggested, stepping forward. Her hand hovered over the wooden door, but before she could knock, it swung open with a creak.

A woman stood in the doorway, her face lined with age but her eyes sparkled with kindness. "You three look weary," she said, her voice warm yet cautious. "Come inside. You're safe here."

Gabriel exchanged glances with Maria and Elara, a mixture of relief and uncertainty flooding him. "Thank you," he said, stepping into the cozy abode, the scent of fresh bread and herbs enveloping them. The room was filled with the comforting glow of candlelight, casting dancing shadows on the walls.

"Sit, sit!" the woman urged, gesturing to a table set with an array of food. "You must be hungry."

They sat down, the weight of their journey pressing heavily on their shoulders. As they began to eat, Gabriel's mind raced, considering their next move. The village seemed idyllic, but he couldn't shake the feeling that they were still being watched.

"What's your name?" Maria asked the woman, breaking the silence.

"Esther," she replied, her eyes twinkling with warmth. "And you are? I don't often see travelers this far into the woods."

"I'm Gabriel, and these are my friends, Maria and Elara," he said, glancing around the cozy room. "We're on a quest. We're being hunted by... well, dark forces."

Esther's expression shifted, a flicker of concern crossing her features. "Dark forces, you say? It's not safe to speak of such things here, dear. The shadows have eyes and ears."

Gabriel felt a chill run down his spine. "What do you mean?"

The woman leaned closer, lowering her voice. "There are those in this village who do not welcome outsiders. They fear the unknown, and sometimes they make deals with the darkness to keep themselves safe."

"What kind of deals?" Elara asked, her voice barely above a whisper.

"The kind that come at a steep price," Esther said, her gaze darting toward the window. "They trade loyalty for safety, and in doing so, they invite shadows into their homes."

Gabriel felt a knot tighten in his stomach. "Is there a way for us to find help here? We need to regroup and figure out how to stop the darkness."

Esther nodded slowly, her expression thoughtful. "There are good people here, but you must be careful. There's a council that governs this village, and they may not take kindly to outsiders seeking refuge."

"We'll be careful," Gabriel assured her, his determination hardening. "We just need to find allies. If we can convince them of our cause, maybe we can prepare for the fight ahead."

Suddenly, a loud knock interrupted their conversation, reverberating through the small room. Gabriel's heart raced as Esther's expression turned to alarm. "Quick, hide!" she urged, darting toward a cupboard in the corner.

Gabriel, Maria, and Elara exchanged panicked glances before diving behind the table, their breaths held in anticipation. The knock echoed again, more insistent this time. "Esther! Open up!" a gruff voice barked from outside.

"Just a moment!" Esther called, her voice steady despite the fear in her eyes. She rushed to the door, taking a deep breath before opening it a crack.

Two men stood on the threshold, their expressions grim. The one in front was tall and broad-shouldered, with a scar running down his cheek that made him look even more menacing. The other was shorter, wearing a cap that shadowed his eyes. "We're looking for strangers. Have you seen anyone pass through?" the tall man demanded.

Esther's face paled as she glanced back toward Gabriel and the others, hidden behind the table. "No, I haven't seen anyone," she said, forcing a smile. "Just the usual villagers."

The man's eyes narrowed, clearly unconvinced. "You'd better not be hiding anyone, Esther. We don't take kindly to outsiders here."

"I swear! No one has been here but the regulars," she insisted, her voice shaking slightly.

"Keep it that way," the tall man said, his tone leaving no room for doubt. "The council has eyes everywhere, and we don't want any trouble."

With that, they turned and left, their footsteps echoing down the path. Gabriel released the breath he had been holding, heart pounding in his chest.

"Thank you," he said, stepping out from behind the table. "You saved us."

Esther looked shaken but relieved. "You must leave soon. They're not going to stop searching, and if they find you, they will bring the darkness down upon us all."

"But we can't just leave," Maria protested, her eyes wide with concern. "We need to find help!"

Esther shook her head. "Help is not what you think it is. You need to be cautious, or you'll find yourselves caught in a web of shadows."

Gabriel felt the weight of her words. "What do you suggest we do?"

37

"There's an old inn at the edge of the village. It's a place where travelers gather, and you may find someone willing to help you there," Esther advised, her eyes darting toward the window again. "But be discreet."

"Thank you, Esther," Gabriel said, gratitude flooding through him. "We won't forget your kindness."

As they prepared to leave, Gabriel felt a surge of determination. The village was rife with danger, but it also held the promise of allies. They had to be smart, cautious, and above all, united.

"Stay close," he instructed as they stepped outside, the cool night air wrapping around them. "We can't afford to be separated."

They moved swiftly through the village, keeping to the shadows as they navigated the narrow cobblestone paths. The sounds of laughter and music drifted through the air, a stark contrast to the tension that hung over them.

As they neared the inn, Gabriel spotted a flicker of movement out of the corner of his eye. A figure stood at the edge of the village square, cloaked in shadow. The hair on the back of his neck stood on end as he instinctively pulled Maria and Elara closer.

"Do you see that?" he whispered, nodding toward the figure.

"Yeah," Elara said, her voice trembling. "What do we do?"

"Let's approach with caution," Gabriel replied, his heart racing. "We need to find out who it is."

As they drew closer, the figure turned, revealing a face shrouded in a dark hood. Gabriel's breath caught in his throat. There was something familiar about that face, something unsettling.

"Gabriel," the figure said, his voice low and gravelly. "I've been looking for you."

Gabriel's heart sank. The shadows had eyes, and it seemed they were now aware of him.

8

Shadows and Whispers

Gabriel's heart pounded in his chest as he stepped closer to the cloaked figure, trying to discern the familiar features obscured by the shadows. The night air felt thick, as if the very atmosphere conspired to choke him with fear. He stole a glance at Maria and Elara, who stood beside him, their expressions a mix of apprehension and curiosity.

"Who are you?" Gabriel demanded, trying to keep his voice steady, but it wavered slightly as he spoke. "What do you want?"

The figure pulled back the hood, revealing a face that sent a jolt of recognition through Gabriel. It was Elias, a former ally from his past—someone he thought he had left behind. "Elias?" Gabriel breathed, his voice barely above a whisper. "What are you doing here?"

Elias looked weary, his eyes shadowed and haunted. "I've come to warn you. The darkness you seek to fight has already taken root here. You're not safe."

"Not safe?" Elara echoed, stepping forward. "What do you mean?"

Elias glanced around nervously, his gaze flickering toward the inn. "There are eyes everywhere. The council has spies, and they are more than willing to turn on anyone they perceive as a threat. You must be careful. They're hunting you."

Gabriel felt a chill run down his spine. "Why would they be hunting us? We're just trying to help."

Elias shook his head. "Help is a double-edged sword in this village. Many fear the unknown, and they see you as harbingers of the darkness they try so hard to keep at bay. You carry the weight of the chalice, and that makes you a target."

"What do we do?" Maria asked, her voice trembling slightly. "We can't just leave; we need to find allies."

"Then you need to be smart about it," Elias replied, his eyes darting around. "Meet me at the old oak tree on the outskirts of the village at midnight. I have information that can help you, but it's too dangerous to talk here."

Gabriel hesitated. "Can we trust you?"

Elias's expression turned serious. "You have no choice. Time is running out. The council is planning something, and if you don't act quickly, you might find yourselves caught in a trap."

"Fine," Gabriel said, his mind racing. "We'll meet you there."

Elias nodded, a look of urgency in his eyes. "Be careful. I'll see you at midnight." With that, he melted back into the shadows, leaving Gabriel and his companions standing in the dim light of the village.

"What do we do now?" Elara asked, her voice barely above a whisper.

"We need to be cautious," Gabriel said, scanning the area for any signs of danger. "Let's get to the inn and lay low until midnight. We'll need our wits about us."

They continued on to the inn, a modest building with a thatched roof and a flickering lantern outside. Gabriel pushed open the door, the hinges creaking ominously. The warm glow inside was inviting, but he could feel the tension in the air. The inn was bustling with activity—villagers were laughing and sharing stories, but the atmosphere felt thick with unspoken fears.

They found a corner table and settled in, ordering some food and drink while keeping their voices low. Gabriel scanned the room, watching the faces around him, trying to gauge who might be an ally and who might be a threat.

"What if we can't trust Elias?" Maria said, her brow furrowed with concern. "What if he's leading us into a trap?"

"We don't have a lot of options," Gabriel replied. "If the council is as dangerous as he says, then we need to be prepared for anything."

The food arrived, but Gabriel found it hard to eat. The tension in his stomach was a knot of fear and uncertainty. The laughter from the other patrons felt distant, almost mocking, and he couldn't shake the feeling that they were being watched.

After they finished eating, they decided to split up and gather more information. "Let's meet back here in an hour," Gabriel suggested. "Stay alert. If anyone asks questions, be vague."

Maria nodded, her expression determined. "I'll check out the bar area. Maybe I can overhear something."

"I'll look around the other patrons," Elara added, her eyes scanning the room.

"I might be able to strike up a conversation."

Gabriel watched as they separated, taking a deep breath to calm the racing thoughts in his mind. He needed to gather information, too, but first, he slipped into the restroom to collect his thoughts. The small room was dimly lit, and as he splashed water on his face, he stared at his reflection. The man looking back at him was worn and weary, but there was a fire in his eyes—a determination to fight the darkness that threatened to consume them.

After a moment, he stepped out, feeling a sense of purpose. He returned to the common area and observed the patrons more closely. A group of men sat in the corner, their voices low and conspiratorial. Gabriel caught snippets of their conversation—words like "the council" and "outsiders" that made his skin crawl.

As he moved closer, he heard one of the men say, "They're bringing trouble with them. We can't let them disrupt the balance."

"Agreed," another man replied. "If we allow them to stay, it will invite the darkness into our homes."

Gabriel's heart raced as he listened. They were talking about him and his friends. He had to find a way to defuse the situation before it spiraled out of control. Just then, he noticed a young woman sitting alone at a table, her expression pensive. She looked familiar, and something about her drew him closer.

"Is everything alright?" Gabriel asked, approaching her table cautiously.

She looked up, surprise flickering in her eyes. "I've seen you before," she said quietly. "You're one of the outsiders they're talking about."

"Do you know me?" Gabriel asked, his pulse quickening. "What do you know about the council?"

"They're dangerous," she replied, glancing around to ensure no one was listening. "If they find out who you are and what you carry, they won't hesitate to act. I've seen what they do to those who threaten their way of life."

"What can we do?" Gabriel pressed, leaning closer. "We're trying to fight against the darkness, but we need allies."

The woman hesitated, biting her lip. "There are some in the village who want to help you, but they're scared. If you can prove that you're not a threat, you might find some support."

"How do we prove that?" Gabriel asked, desperation creeping into his voice.

"By showing them that you're willing to fight for the village, to protect it from the shadows. There's a meeting tonight after the council convenes. If you can get in there and convince them you're on their side, it might buy you some time."

Gabriel felt a surge of hope mixed with fear. "Thank you," he said earnestly. "What's your name?"

"Clara," she replied, her gaze steady. "But you have to be careful. The council is always watching, and if they see you talking to me—"

Gabriel nodded, urgency coursing through him. "I understand. I'll be cautious."

As he stood to leave, the sound of heavy footsteps echoed behind him. Gabriel turned just in time to see the tall man from earlier striding toward him, flanked by two others. "There you are," the man said, his voice dripping with menace. "We've been looking for you."

A cold wave of fear washed over Gabriel. He was caught between the council's watchful eyes and the shadows lurking just beyond the light. The game had changed, and he could feel the walls closing in around him. He had to think fast, or he would be swallowed by the very darkness he sought to fight.

9

The Council's Gaze

The air in the inn thickened with tension as the tall man approached, his shadow stretching across Gabriel like a dark cloud. The laughter and chatter of the patrons faded into a hushed murmur, and Gabriel could feel the weight of dozens of eyes upon him. A sinking feeling settled in his stomach, and every instinct screamed at him to run, but he knew he had to stand his ground.

"Gabriel, was it?" the man sneered, crossing his arms over his broad chest. "You really shouldn't be wandering around here unguarded."

Gabriel swallowed hard, forcing himself to meet the man's piercing gaze. "I'm just having a conversation," he replied, his voice steadier than he felt. "Is that against the rules?"

The man chuckled, but it lacked any humor. "In this village, everything is scrutinized. Especially when it comes to outsiders." He gestured toward Clara, who sat frozen at the table, her eyes wide with fear. "You don't want to be seen with her. She's got a reputation for stirring trouble."

"I'm not stirring anything," Clara retorted, her voice shaking slightly. "I'm just trying to help."

"Help?" the man scoffed, taking a step closer. "What kind of help do you think a couple of lost souls can offer? You don't belong here. The council won't take kindly to your presence, especially not after what happened last time."

Gabriel's heart raced. "What happened last time?" he asked, curiosity piqued despite the danger.

The man leaned in, lowering his voice. "A band of travelers like you came through, claiming to fight against the darkness. They were met with suspicion, and the council decided it was easier to get rid of them than to take any chances. We don't need that kind of disruption in our lives."

Fear twisted in Gabriel's gut. "What did they do?" he pressed, unable to look away from the man's hardened features.

"They disappeared," the man said flatly. "No one knows what happened to them, and we intend to keep it that way. You would be wise to remember that."

As he turned to leave, Gabriel felt a rush of adrenaline. "Wait," he called out, determination fueling his voice. "I'm not like them. I'm here to protect this village from the very darkness you're afraid of."

The man stopped and looked back, skepticism etched on his face. "Is that so?"

Gabriel took a step forward, heart racing. "Yes. I've seen what's lurking in the shadows, and I refuse to let it take root here."

The man's expression shifted, a flicker of interest crossing his features. "You're either very brave or very foolish. Either way, you'll need more than words to convince the council of your intentions."

"I'm willing to do whatever it takes," Gabriel said, desperation creeping into his tone.

"Then you should prepare yourself," the man replied, his voice cold. "The council will meet tonight, and they will scrutinize every word you say. They are not known for their mercy."

With that, he turned on his heel and strode away, leaving Gabriel with a churning mix of anxiety and determination. He had to act quickly, and the clock was ticking. He scanned the room for Maria and Elara, but the gathering crowd had shifted, obscuring his view.

"Gabriel?" Clara's voice broke through his thoughts, and he turned to see her looking at him intently. "You need to leave now."

"What do you mean?" Gabriel asked, bewildered.

"They're going to be watching you," she replied urgently. "You need to find a way to warn your friends without alerting the council."

"How do I do that?" he asked, glancing around to make sure no one was eavesdropping.

"There's a back exit to this inn," Clara said, her voice low. "You can slip out and meet them before it's too late. But you have to hurry."

Gabriel hesitated for a moment, weighing his options. He knew that if he stayed here much longer, the council's spies would catch on to him. "Okay, I'll go," he decided, steeling himself. "But I need you to be careful too. If they find you—"

"I'll be fine," she said, a determined glint in her eyes. "Just go."

Gabriel took one last look around the inn, then nodded and slipped through the door Clara indicated. The cool night air hit him like a wave as he emerged into the alley behind the inn, a sense of urgency propelling him forward.

He sprinted down the dimly lit path, the sounds of the village fading behind him. Each step felt heavy with the weight of what lay ahead. He needed to warn Maria and Elara and figure out a plan before the council meeting began.

As he rounded a corner, he spotted a flicker of light up ahead—Maria and Elara huddled together, their expressions tense. Relief washed over him, and he quickened his pace, calling out their names.

"Gabriel!" Maria exclaimed, her eyes widening. "We were worried about you!"

"I ran into some trouble," he said, glancing around to ensure they were alone. "We need to move. The council is looking for us, and we don't have much time."

"What do we do?" Elara asked, her voice shaking. "Are we in danger?"

Gabriel nodded, his heart racing. "The tall man warned me about what happened to others like us. If we don't convince the council that we're here to help, we could end up like them—disappeared."

"What's the plan?" Maria asked, determination etched on her face.

"We need to get to the council meeting before it starts," Gabriel replied, his mind racing. "Clara said if we can prove our intentions, we might find allies. We can't let fear dictate our choices."

"Right," Elara said, taking a deep breath. "Let's go."

They made their way through the village, moving quickly but cautiously.

Gabriel's heart pounded in his chest as he led the way, each shadow feeling more threatening than the last. The moon hung high in the sky, casting an eerie light over the cobblestone streets.

As they neared the town hall, the air grew thick with anticipation. The building loomed ahead, its windows glowing with flickering candlelight. Gabriel could feel the weight of the council's gaze even before they stepped inside.

"Remember, stay close and don't draw attention to yourselves," Gabriel instructed, his voice low but steady.

They entered the hall, and the atmosphere shifted. A long table occupied the center of the room, where several villagers sat, their expressions stern and watchful. The air crackled with tension, and Gabriel felt a shiver run down his spine.

"Gabriel!" a voice called from across the room. It was Esther, the woman who had taken them in earlier. "You made it."

"Esther," Gabriel replied, relief flooding through him. "We need to speak to the council."

"Good," she said, moving closer. "They've been waiting for you."

As they approached the council table, Gabriel's heart raced. The council members looked at them with a mix of suspicion and curiosity. He could feel their eyes boring into him, dissecting his every move.

"Why have you come here?" one of the council members demanded, a woman with sharp features and a piercing gaze.

Gabriel took a deep breath, gathering his courage. "We're here to help. We've seen the darkness that threatens this village, and we refuse to stand by and let it take root."

"Help?" the woman scoffed. "You expect us to trust you? Outsiders have brought nothing but trouble in the past."

"I know the risks," Gabriel replied, his voice firm. "But we have the knowledge and the skills to fight back against the shadows. If you give us a chance, we can prove our worth."

The council exchanged wary glances, and Gabriel could feel the tension in the room thickening. This was it—the moment that would determine their fate.

"Prove your worth, then," the woman said, her tone icy. "What can you do that we cannot?"

Gabriel glanced at Maria and Elara, their eyes filled with a mix of fear and determination. He had to convince them; their lives depended on it.

"If you allow us to work together, we can show you the strategies we've developed. We've fought against the darkness before, and we know how to face it head-on," he said, his voice growing stronger with conviction.

The council members continued to deliberate, their expressions unreadable. Gabriel's heart raced as he awaited their decision, knowing that every moment they hesitated brought them closer to the edge of danger.

Finally, the woman leaned forward, her eyes narrowing. "Very well. You have one chance to prove yourselves. But know this: if you fail, it will be the end of you."

Gabriel nodded, steeling himself for the challenge ahead. They had entered the lion's den, but he wouldn't back down now. They were in the fight of their lives, and the fate of the village rested squarely on their shoulders.

10

The Test of Resolve

The council chamber felt like a cauldron of simmering tension, and Gabriel could sense the collective doubt from the gathered villagers. As the council's gaze remained fixed on him, he took a deep breath, steeling himself for the challenges ahead. The flickering candles cast shadows on the walls, creating a dance of light and dark that seemed to reflect the very struggle they were about to embark on.

"Prove yourselves," the sharp-featured council member declared, her voice slicing through the charged atmosphere. "You have until dawn to show us you're not a threat. What do you propose?"

Gabriel exchanged glances with Maria and Elara, his mind racing. He felt the weight of their expectations resting heavily on his shoulders. "We need to confront the darkness directly. If it's as pervasive as we believe, we can draw it out and face it together."

"Face it?" another council member interjected, a burly man with a bushy beard. "And what if it consumes you? What then?"

"We'll face it with knowledge and strategy," Gabriel replied, his voice steady despite the fear coursing through him. "We know the signs of its presence and can use our skills to protect the village. We need your support—both in manpower and resources."

The council exchanged glances again, their skepticism palpable. Gabriel could feel his heart pounding in his chest, each beat echoing the urgency of the moment. "If you want to win the villagers' trust, you must first prove you can protect them," the woman continued, leaning forward. "Gather your strength and be ready for a confrontation. But know this: failure is not an option."

"Then let's prepare," Gabriel said, determination flooding his voice. "If we are to confront this darkness, we need to know its secrets. We should start by visiting the old ruins on the outskirts of the village. It's said that the shadows gather there, and perhaps we can find clues about their movements."

The council murmured among themselves, and Gabriel took the opportunity to address the villagers gathered behind him. "I know you are scared," he said, his voice rising above the chatter. "But I promise you, we will do everything we can to protect this village. The darkness we face is not just a threat to us; it is a threat to all of you. If we stand together, we can drive it away."

A few heads nodded, but many remained skeptical, their expressions hard and unyielding. Gabriel felt a pang of frustration but pushed it aside. He had to focus on the task ahead.

"We need to act quickly," he urged. "The longer we wait, the stronger the darkness will become. We must work through the night to prepare for the dawn."

"Very well," the council woman finally said, her voice still cool. "You have until the first light. Gather your allies, prepare your tools, and return to us before dawn."

With that, the meeting was adjourned, and Gabriel felt the weight of their challenge pressing down on him as he turned to Maria and Elara. "We need to rally as many villagers as we can. The more we have on our side, the better our chances."

They left the council chamber and stepped into the cool night air, the stars above twinkling like distant eyes watching their every move. The streets were quiet, but an undercurrent of fear lingered. Gabriel could feel it in the way the villagers kept their doors tightly shut, peeking through the cracks as if expecting shadows to leap out at them.

"Where do we start?" Maria asked, her brow furrowed with concern.

"There's a gathering spot at the edge of the village, near the marketplace," Gabriel suggested. "We can meet there and see who's willing to join us."

The three of them moved quickly through the darkened streets, their footsteps muffled against the cobblestones. As they neared the marketplace, they could see a few villagers lingering near the stalls, whispering among themselves.

"Let me handle this," Gabriel said, his heart racing. He stepped forward, clearing his throat to draw attention. "Everyone, listen! We're gathering a group to confront the darkness that threatens our village. We need your strength and support!"

The villagers turned to him, their expressions a mix of curiosity and skepticism. "And what makes you think you can stop it?" an elderly woman called out, her voice sharp. "We've seen what happens to those who try."

"We're not trying to go in blindly," Gabriel replied, raising his hands to calm the crowd. "We have knowledge and skills that can help us fight back. We've faced the darkness before, and we're willing to do it again for the sake of this village. But we need your help. Together, we stand a chance."

"I'd rather keep my family safe than chase shadows," a burly man said, crossing his arms defiantly.

Gabriel felt his heart sink at the resistance, but he couldn't give up now. "You can keep your family safe by standing with us!" he implored. "If we allow fear to control us, the darkness will consume us all. This is our chance to fight back."

The crowd murmured, and Gabriel could see a flicker of uncertainty in their eyes. "We can't afford to lose more people," Elara spoke up, stepping beside Gabriel. "We've already lost so many to this threat. This is our opportunity to protect what we love."

Gabriel nodded, encouraged by her words. "If you don't believe us, then join us at the old ruins. You can see for yourself the strength we carry. We will face the darkness together."

Slowly, a few villagers stepped forward, glancing at one another as if seeking silent approval. "I'll come," a middle-aged man said, his voice steady. "My brother is still missing. I want to find out what happened."

"I'll come too," a young woman added, her expression fierce. "I refuse to live in fear any longer."

As more voices began to chime in, Gabriel felt a surge of hope. They were starting to rally, and the weight of their fear began to lift, replaced by a shared sense of purpose.

"Let's meet at the ruins in an hour," Gabriel said, his voice rising above the murmurs. "We need to prepare, and we need everyone's strength. We can't do this alone."

As the villagers began to disperse and gather their things, Maria and Elara exchanged determined glances. "We have to find Clara," Elara said, urgency in her voice. "She deserves to be part of this."

"Right," Gabriel agreed. "Let's split up and meet back at the ruins. We'll gather as many people as we can."

With a sense of purpose guiding them, they set off in different directions. Gabriel moved swiftly through the village, his heart racing as he thought of the task ahead. He needed to gather strength from every corner of the village, and the weight of the darkness pressed heavily on his shoulders.

After a few tense encounters, he managed to rally several more villagers, each with their own reasons for joining the fight. When he finally found Clara at her home, she looked surprised but determined. "I heard about the meeting," she said, her eyes shining with resolve. "I want to help."

"Thank you," Gabriel said, relief flooding through him. "We need all the strength we can gather. Meet us at the ruins in an hour."

As night deepened and stars twinkled above, the villagers began to converge at the old ruins. Gabriel stood at the front, his heart pounding in his chest as he watched them gather. They were scared, but determination flickered in their eyes.

"This is it," he thought, steeling himself. "This is our chance to confront the darkness."

As the last of the villagers arrived, Gabriel could see the mixture of fear and courage in their faces. He took a deep breath, preparing to address them. "We've all come here for a reason. The shadows are closing in, and we need to face them together. We may not know what lies ahead, but we are stronger when we stand united."

As the first light of dawn began to break over the horizon, Gabriel felt a sense of resolve wash over him. They were ready to confront whatever awaited them. The time for doubt had passed; they would stand together against the darkness, and no matter what happened, they would fight for their village, for their loved ones, and for their very lives.

11

Into the Abyss

The air was charged with anticipation as dawn's first light broke over the horizon, casting long shadows through the ancient trees surrounding the ruins. Gabriel stood at the forefront of the gathered villagers, his heart racing. The ruins loomed ahead like a gaping maw, beckoning them to venture into the unknown. Whispers of fear floated on the morning breeze, but he could also sense a flicker of determination igniting within the crowd. They were ready, and yet the weight of uncertainty loomed over them like a storm cloud.

"Stay close," Gabriel instructed, turning to face the assembled villagers. "The darkness we face may manifest in ways we cannot predict. Trust in each other, and do not let fear take hold."

Clara stepped beside him, her face pale but resolute. "We've heard stories of these ruins. If there are any remnants of the darkness, it's likely to be here." She glanced toward the dilapidated stone structures, their edges softened by creeping vines. "We must be prepared for anything."

As they approached the ruins, a chill swept through the air, raising the hairs on Gabriel's arms. The stone walls appeared to absorb the light, casting an oppressive gloom around them. The villagers shifted uneasily, exchanging glances that spoke volumes of their trepidation. Gabriel felt their fear but also the resolve beneath it. They were all willing to confront the shadows together.

With each step, the path grew narrower, overgrown with weeds and debris, and the sunlight began to fade behind the ancient stone walls. Gabriel took a deep breath, forcing himself to focus. He led the way inside, the sound of crunching leaves and twigs beneath their feet punctuating the silence.

Inside the ruins, the atmosphere thickened, heavy with the scent of damp earth and moss. Shadows danced along the walls, twisted and warped by the flickering light. Gabriel could almost hear the whispers of the past echoing in his mind, tales of those who had come before him and failed to return.

"Keep your eyes peeled," he whispered to Maria and Elara as they ventured deeper into the structure. "We must stay vigilant."

As they moved further in, they came to a central chamber, illuminated by beams of sunlight that pierced through cracks in the stone ceiling. At the heart of the room lay an altar, ancient and covered in dark, creeping vines. Gabriel felt a pull toward it, an inexplicable urge that sent a shiver down his spine.

"This is where they performed their rituals," Clara murmured, stepping closer to the altar. "It's said that those who sought power often met their doom here."

As Clara reached out to touch the surface, Gabriel called out, "Wait! We need to be careful. We don't know what could be awakened."

But Clara was already brushing the vines aside, revealing intricate carvings etched into the stone. Symbols that spoke of darkness and despair, of those who had come seeking strength but found only ruin. The air around them crackled with energy, and Gabriel felt a sense of foreboding settle over the group.

Suddenly, a low growl echoed through the chamber, reverberating off the walls. The villagers froze, eyes wide with fear as they turned toward the sound. Gabriel's heart raced; they weren't alone.

"What was that?" Elara whispered, her voice trembling.

"I don't know," Gabriel replied, his pulse quickening. "But we need to be ready."

The growl grew louder, a guttural rumble that sent chills down Gabriel's spine. From the shadows emerged a figure, hulking and twisted, its eyes glowing with an eerie light. It moved with an unnatural grace, like a predator stalking its prey. The villagers gasped, stepping back, and Gabriel felt the weight of their fear.

"Form a line!" Gabriel shouted, trying to keep his voice steady. "Stay together!"

The creature paused, its gaze sweeping over the group, lingering on Gabriel. A low rumble emanated from its throat, and it lunged forward with terrifying speed.

"Now!" Gabriel yelled, raising his weapon as the villagers scrambled to form a defensive line. Clara, Maria, and Elara stood shoulder to shoulder, their faces set with determination.

As the creature lunged, Gabriel swung his weapon, but it sailed through the air, connecting with nothing but shadows. The creature vanished and reappeared behind him, its breath hot against his neck.

"Watch out!" Elara screamed, but it was too late. The creature struck, sending

Gabriel sprawling to the ground.

The world tilted, and for a moment, everything was a blur. Gabriel felt a searing pain in his side as he scrambled to regain his footing. The villagers shouted, chaos erupting around him. He pushed himself up, adrenaline surging through his veins, and spotted Clara battling the creature.

"Clara, stay back!" he shouted, his voice cutting through the panic.

But Clara was relentless, striking at the creature with fierce determination. She landed a blow, but it only seemed to anger the beast. It turned its attention toward her, its glowing eyes narrowing as it prepared to attack.

"No!" Gabriel yelled, rushing forward. He knew they couldn't afford to lose anyone now. He needed to protect them all.

With a burst of energy, he tackled the creature, forcing it back into the shadows. The air around them crackled as the darkness seemed to pulse and swirl. He could hear the whispers, the voices of those who had come before, urging him to succumb to despair.

But he wouldn't give in. Not now, not ever.

"Everyone, focus!" he called out, rallying the villagers. "We need to work together!"

As he battled the creature, the villagers found their courage, rallying behind him. They attacked as one, their fear transformed into resolve. Gabriel felt the energy shift as they joined forces, each blow striking true against the darkness that threatened to consume them.

The creature howled, a piercing sound that echoed through the chamber, and in that moment, Gabriel saw its weakness—a flicker of doubt in its eyes. It was terrified, just as they were.

"Keep pressing!" he urged, fueled by a newfound determination. "We can drive it back!"

With every strike, they pushed the creature further, forcing it to retreat. The air buzzed with a strange energy, and the darkness around them began to dissipate, unraveling like threads of a fraying tapestry.

But then, just as victory seemed within reach, the creature let out a final, deafening roar that shook the very stones beneath their feet. It surged forward, desperate and angry, a tide of darkness threatening to engulf them all.

"Hold the line!" Gabriel shouted, determination igniting within him. "We will not back down!"

With one final surge, the villagers rallied together, and Gabriel led the charge. They struck with everything they had, a cacophony of resolve and courage resonating through the chamber. Light pushed back against the shadows, illuminating the dark corners of the ruins.

As the creature recoiled, Gabriel seized the moment. He drew upon every ounce of strength and courage, channeling it into a single strike aimed at the heart of the darkness. The impact sent shockwaves through the air, and the creature howled in agony as it was engulfed by brilliant light.

And then, silence fell. The light flickered and faded, and the creature vanished, leaving behind only a heavy stillness. The villagers stood panting, their faces a mix of disbelief and relief. Gabriel looked around at them, seeing the shared triumph in their eyes.

"We did it," Clara whispered, tears glistening in her eyes. "We faced the darkness."

Gabriel felt a wave of exhaustion wash over him, but beneath it was a profound sense of achievement. They had confronted the abyss and emerged victorious. But as he surveyed the ruins, he couldn't shake the feeling that this was only the beginning. There were more shadows lurking, and their journey was far from over.

"Let's regroup and assess the situation," he said, his voice steady. "We need to understand what just happened and prepare for whatever comes next. This fight isn't over yet."

As they gathered their breaths and strength, the first rays of sunlight pierced through the ruins, illuminating the once-shadowed chamber. The darkness had retreated, but Gabriel knew it was merely a temporary reprieve. Together, they would continue to stand against the shadows, ready to embrace the challenges ahead, united in their resolve to protect their village and one another.

12

The Gathering Storm

The ruins were eerily quiet after the battle, a stillness settling over the space like a thick fog. Gabriel stood at the center of the chamber, breathless and aching from the confrontation. Sunlight streamed through the cracks in the stone above, illuminating the altar where they had faced the darkness. The carved symbols now looked different—less menacing, perhaps, as if their meaning had shifted from foreboding to a testament of their triumph.

But the victory felt hollow. The echoes of the creature's howl still reverberated in his mind, reminding him that this battle was just one of many to come. He turned to the gathered villagers, their faces still flushed with adrenaline, a mix of relief and fear etched in their expressions. Clara wiped her brow, her hands trembling slightly as she surveyed the ruins, her gaze lingering on the shadows that still lurked at the edges of the chamber.

"Is it really over?" Clara asked, her voice barely above a whisper. "Did we truly drive it away?"

Gabriel swallowed hard, struggling to find the right words. "For now, yes," he said, but doubt crept into his voice. "But we need to understand what we're up against. That creature was only a manifestation of something much larger and more insidious."

"We need to prepare for the worst," Elara chimed in, her face pale but resolute. "What if there are more of them? What if they come back in greater numbers?"

A murmur of agreement rippled through the group, and Gabriel felt a weight settle on his shoulders. He could sense the fear in the air, a palpable tension that clung to them like the dampness of the ruins. "We need to gather more information about the darkness," he said firmly. "And that means heading back to the village and speaking to the elders. They may have insights or histories that can guide us."

"Right," Clara said, determination glinting in her eyes. "We should also gather supplies. We need weapons, food, and any tools that might help us in case we need to fight again."

As they began to regroup and organize, Gabriel's mind raced. He felt the urgency of their situation, the ticking clock of impending danger. The sun was beginning to rise higher, casting shadows that stretched and warped across the ancient stone. The villagers moved with purpose, but he could sense the undercurrent of anxiety.

"Let's not waste any more time," Gabriel urged. "We'll head back to the village and share what we've learned. We need to prepare everyone for what's to come."

The journey back to the village was tense, the silence between them filled with unspoken fears. As they navigated the winding path, the sounds of nature felt muted, as if the world itself was holding its breath. Gabriel's heart raced with every step, a sense of foreboding weighing heavily on him.

When they finally reached the village, the first rays of morning sunlight illuminated the homes, casting a warm glow that belied the tension in the air. Villagers were moving about, but their eyes held a wariness that spoke of lingering fear. As Gabriel and his group approached, they were met with a mix of curiosity and apprehension.

"Did you confront it?" a villager called out, stepping forward. His face was lined with worry. "Are you safe?"

"We faced a creature of the darkness," Gabriel replied, standing tall to address the crowd. "And we drove it back for now. But this is just the beginning. We need your help."

A ripple of unease swept through the villagers. "What do you mean?" another voice asked, tinged with skepticism.

"The darkness is not gone," Clara interjected, stepping forward beside Gabriel. "It's still out there, and it may return stronger than before. We need to prepare—gather supplies, fortify our defenses, and share our knowledge of the past."

As they spoke, Gabriel could see the fear in their eyes, the weight of uncertainty hanging heavily over them. He could feel the collective anxiety, and he knew they had to act quickly to harness that fear and transform it into resolve.

"We need to convene the elders," Gabriel said, glancing at Clara and Elara for support. "They may have information about the darkness that can help us. We must understand what we're dealing with if we're to fight it."

The villagers nodded slowly, murmurs of agreement growing louder. "Let's gather everyone at the town hall," one of the elders suggested, a woman with gray hair and a gaze that seemed to see through the chaos. "We need to share what we know and devise a plan."

The group made their way to the town hall, a modest building that stood at the heart of the village. As they entered, the tension in the air was palpable, every eye fixed on Gabriel and his companions. They could feel the weight of expectation pressing down on them, the villagers seeking hope in the midst of fear.

Gabriel stepped forward, raising his hands to silence the crowd. "Thank you for gathering on such short notice. We have faced a manifestation of the darkness, and while we fought it off, we cannot underestimate what lies ahead. We must come together as a community if we are to protect ourselves."

The elders exchanged worried glances, their expressions grim. "What do you propose?" the woman with gray hair asked.

"We need to strengthen our defenses, gather supplies, and share our knowledge," Gabriel replied. "The darkness feeds on fear and division. If we stand united, we can confront it together."

The elders nodded, and Gabriel could sense a flicker of hope beginning to spread among the villagers. "We need to fortify our borders, set up watch points, and establish a plan for what to do if the darkness returns," Clara added, her voice steady.

"Agreed," one of the elders spoke up, his brow furrowed in thought. "But we must also be cautious. We don't know how the darkness will respond to our preparations. It may strike at our weakest points."

Gabriel nodded, his mind racing with possibilities. "Then we need to identify those points now. We should divide into groups—some to gather supplies, others to establish defenses. We can't afford to wait."

As discussions unfolded, Gabriel felt a swell of determination rise within him. The villagers were beginning to unite, their fears coalescing into a sense of purpose. They moved about the hall, forming plans and sharing ideas, and he watched as the energy in the room shifted from despair to resolve.

Suddenly, a loud crash echoed from outside, followed by frantic shouting. The villagers froze, fear creeping back into their expressions. Gabriel's heart raced as he exchanged glances with Clara and Elara. "Stay here!" he commanded, his voice firm. "I'll see what's happening."

He dashed toward the door, the weight of dread heavy in his chest. The villagers followed, crowding behind him as he stepped outside. The scene before him was chaos. Several villagers were attempting to hold back a massive barricade of fallen trees and debris that had inexplicably crashed into the village square, blocking access to the outer roads.

"What happened?" Gabriel shouted over the commotion.

"We were checking the perimeter!" one of the men replied, breathless. "Then we heard a noise, and everything just... fell!"

A low rumble vibrated through the ground, sending tremors of fear coursing through the gathered villagers. The ground quaked beneath them, and an unnatural chill swept through the air. The sky darkened, clouds swirling ominously overhead as if the very heavens were responding to the presence of the darkness.

Gabriel's pulse quickened as he scanned the area, feeling the weight of impending danger. "We need to clear this debris—now!" he shouted, rallying the villagers to action.

As they worked together to move the fallen trees and barricades, a growing sense of dread settled in Gabriel's gut. He couldn't shake the feeling that the darkness was drawing closer, watching, waiting for the perfect moment to strike.

Just as they cleared the last of the debris, a guttural growl resonated through the village, sending a wave of terror through the crowd. Gabriel turned to face the sound, dread pooling in his stomach. Shadows twisted and writhed at the edges of the square, coalescing into dark figures that seemed to pulsate with malevolence.

"They're here!" a villager screamed, panic rising in the air. The crowd erupted into chaos, but Gabriel felt a strange calm wash over him. This was what they had prepared for; they had faced the darkness once, and they could do it again.

"Stay together!" Gabriel shouted, his voice cutting through the fear. "We can fight this!"

The villagers rallied behind him, fear transforming into resolve as they prepared to face the encroaching shadows. The figures grew larger, their glowing eyes piercing through the dimness as they advanced, but Gabriel stood firm. This was their moment to confront the darkness, to unite against the fear that threatened to tear them apart.

As the shadows closed in, Gabriel raised his weapon, heart racing, ready to face whatever horrors awaited them. This time, they would not back down. The battle for their village had begun anew, and they would fight together, determined to stand strong against the gathering storm.

Milton Keynes UK
Ingram Content Group UK Ltd.
UKHW020320021124
450424UK00013B/1356

9 788005 986833